THE ELEPHANT LETTERS

THE STORY OF BILLY AND KANI

THE ELEPHANT LETTERS

THE STORY OF BILLY AND KANI

by G.A. Bradshaw

Illustrations by Joyce VanDeWater

Awakeling

Press

Published by Awakeling Press

ISBN 978-0-692-20996-7

Print-ready document preparation by bookow.com

Dedicated to Lorraine Donlon,
the Students of East Rockaway, and
Children of All Animals Around the World

Contents

Foreword

Dr. Dame Daphne Sheldrick, DBE, MBE. MBS, DVMS
Chairperson, The David Sheldrick Wildlife Trust

Every child that reads the very moving story of little Billy and Kani will be able to relate to the fact that "Elephants are just like us," which is something that Dr. Gay Bradshaw has publicly stated. To this I would add "in fact, better than us," for they can teach us Humans a great deal about caring and nurturing, and also about forgiveness. It is important to understand that at any age an Elephant child duplicates a Human child in terms of age. They develop at the same pace as us, (although during their three years of milk-dependent infancy they are much more "together" than a Human child of that age); they reach puberty and adulthood at the same age as us, and they have been endowed with the same expected lifespan. Sadly though, in this day and age, few are afforded the privilege of dying of old age, as do most Humans, due to the demand for their ivory teeth.

In childhood they can be mischievous just like Human children, playing deliberate pranks on one another. They have likes and dislikes amongst their peers, just like us, forming strong bonds of friendship, just like Human children, with an even more enduring sense of "family" than ourselves.

Rearing their orphaned babies into adulthood has provided us with a unique insight into the intelligence of these wonderful and compassionate animals, who have been endowed with the best Human traits and few of the bad. In their fragile infancy, we have healed their heartache as well as their wounds, handling them only with tenderness and kindness, as would their Elephant family. This has brought those of us who are privileged to represent their Human surrogate family rich rewards in terms of a unique understanding of the way Elephants feel and think, how they behave towards one another, and how they live in harmony with one another, respecting rank and age. I have regarded it as my duty to bear witness to the very Human emotional characteristics of Elephants, to their astonishing sense of responsibility, even in infancy, to their amazing powers of communication, and to their mysterious perception, which borders on magic and defies Human logic.

Unlike us, Elephants are born with an imprinted genetic memory of aspects important to survival and of how to fulfill their function within Nature. Elephants "never forget," so their forgiveness of the terrible injustices we Humans have done to their kind – robbing them of their loved ones simply for a tooth – is particularly touching. Those of us who know them intimately cannot escape a sense of deep shame for such wicked injustice.

As a scientist and psychologist Gay Bradshaw's insight into the Elephant psyche has been an important milestone within the scientific world to counter the myth that precludes "anthropomorphism." To understand an Elephant, one must be "anthropomorphic," because Elephants are emotionally identical to ourselves. They grieve and mourn the loss of a loved one just as deeply as do we, and their capacity for love is humbling.

It has been a wondrous experience to watch over 140 orphaned infant African Elephants grow day by day, to understand their minds and their moods, and ultimately to be able to experience the greatest reward of all, the privilege of being shown an ex orphan's wild-born baby and, as part of the "family," allowed access to her as she shelters beneath her mother.

To be able to walk within an Elephant herd when an ex Orphan Mother brings back her newborn baby, surrounded by Elephant Carers, simply to proudly show a Human is surely a reward that cannot be matched. It is a "thank you" for the years of nurturing and care involved in getting the Mother and the Carers to that point.

All our orphans are given the freedom of choice to return to where they rightly belong as soon as they feel ready to do so, for it is their birthright to be able to live amongst their wild kin in an area that can offer such great wanderers the space they need for a quality of life in wild terms. The Call of the Wild is very strong, and respecting that need is the greatest gift any Human can give an Elephant – that along with protection and understanding, and the enduring respect and love of which this iconic species is worthy. *The Elephant Letters* will bring this important message to children around the world.

CHAPTER I

The Brown Parcel

It was a beautiful summer night in Africa. Stars glittered in the velvet sky and the moon spread her silver blanket across the plain. There, under the arching form of a giant fig tree stood an old Elephant. His body was wrinkled and grey and his white tusks were so long that they nearly touched the ground. He was Umkhulu, Grandfather of the Elephants.

Next to the tip of the Old Bull's long trunk, lay a small square parcel. It was wrapped in brown paper and covered with stamps from many countries. Young Elephants gathered in a circle at Umkhulu's feet. Their little trunks waved in excitement as they pushed and pulled each other, trying to get closer to the mysterious package. "Grandfather, Grandfather!" they trumpeted, "Please open the package! Please open the package so we can see what's inside!"

But despite the young Elephants' pleas, Umkhulu would not answer. He remained silent and unmoving. Was that a tear, the young Elephants wondered, in the corner of the Old Bull's eye?

What was it that made the big strong Elephant so quiet and sad? Without speaking, Umkhulu turned away. He walked slowly toward the forest edge, his heavy trunk swaying. The young Elephants fell silent as they watched the Old Bull melt into the trees and disappear from sight. Their heads and trunks hung low in disappointment. Finally, after making sure that Umkhulu was not coming back, they left the fig tree to find a place to sleep for the night.
When the young Elephants woke the following day, Umkhulu had not returned. They were afraid and their faces creased with worry. There were hunters and soldiers who stalked the hills in search of Elephants, like the Old Bull, whose magnificent tusks were prized for their ivory.

The next day, there was still no sign of Umkhulu. Anxiously, the young Elephants went to find sweet roots and leaves and drink trunkfulls of water at the river. The day passed slowly. The sky was empty, the bright blue expanse broken only by the arc of eagles flying high above.

Later, as the sun began his travel down to Earth, the young Elephants prepared for night. But before going to bed, they looked once more for the Old Bull. Walking in single file, each holding the tail of the one in front with his trunk, they climbed up the hilltop to the giant fig tree. Suddenly, they saw Umkhulu! The Old Bull was back! The young Elephants ran toward him trumpeting, "Umkhulu! Umkhulu! Grandfather! Grandfather! You are back!"
The Old Bull smiled, his dark brown eyes crinkling with affection. He waved his big strong trunk and, in a deep warm voice, called the young Elephants to gather round. They quickly obeyed. One by one, they trotted over to the fig tree and sat in a circle at Umkhulu's feet. Quietly, they waited.

The Old Bull loomed like a silent grey mountain. The only sounds to be heard were cicadas singing and lions roaring in the distance.

After a few minutes, the Old Elephant raised his heavy head.

Slowly making his way around the circle, he looked into the eyes of each young Elephant, until he came to the youngest sitting by his side, a baby no more than two years old. Only then did the Old Bull bring out the mysterious parcel.

Gently, he laid it on the ground, and using the delicate tip of his trunk, pulled on the string. The brown paper fell away. The young Elephants whispered to each other excitedly and pushed forward to see what was inside. Umkhulu held up his trunk and spoke:

"My Children, you are part of a great civilization whose mighty trunk once stretched across all of Africa from sea to sea. Elephants are a peaceful people. Since time began, we have lived in harmony with Humans and other Animals. We have shared the land and cared for each other's families so that everyone had plenty of food and water.

Now, things have changed. Humans have grown unkind. They take things that were never theirs. They have robbed the land leaving other Animals with nothing to eat and nowhere to live. The mighty Elephant must walk the forest in the dead of night so as not to be seen. Our Bulls and Matriarchs are killed for their ivory tusks and our children are stolen and taken away to zoos and circuses.

Young Ones, Elephants are in danger! We must stand together and restore peace on Earth! Some of you are still very young and need to stay with your Mothers and Aunties. But others are of an age when they can step forward to join the adult Elephants.

The Elders and I will teach you. You must learn how to heal the Human unhappiness that has brought such pain and grief. Elephants cannot live in peace and dignity until Humans return to the Old Ways.

Tonight, however, you may sit under moonlit skies without fear. I will tell you the story of two brave elephants, Imenti and Kani. They were cousins born on the same morning in the beautiful land of Kenya. They played in the tall green grass. At night, they dreamed under the shining moon and stars.

But one day, Humans captured Imenti and carried him off to a zoo in a land far away. They even took away his Elephant name and called him Billy. But they could not take away the love the cousins shared. The two young Elephants never forgot each other and they kept their friendship by sending letters over the many years. It is my hope that the stories of Billy and Kani will teach you how to save our people so that Humans can live with Elephants in harmony and peace again. May the Elephant Letters be your guide."

The Old Bull spoke no more. Cicadas sang and the stars shone bright. The young Elephants had grown silent.

XOXO

The older ones reached out to hold the trunks of the babies who looked frightened. Then, without a word, the Old Bull uncurled his trunk and lifted off the brown parcel lid.

There, inside, were two stacks of envelopes, some white, some yellowed, others brown and smudged with dirt. The envelopes looked old, almost as old as Umkhulu himself. After a few minutes, the Old Bull picked up an envelope that lay on the top of the pile and pulled out a letter. Pushing the folded paper flat with his trunk, he took a deep breath and began to read.

CHAPTER II

Now We Are Seven

Dear Billy,

Hello, hello, hello and happy birthday! Today we are seven years old! I can't believe a whole year has gone by! So much happens on the Savanna every day, it's hard to keep track of time. This year Mama and the Aunties surprised me by taking us all to the river for my birthday party. The whole family was there – Grandmama, Mama, Auntie Vivi, Auntie B., Auntie Eleanor, Mishak, Barbara, Amos, Julius, and Jospeh! We spent the whole day splashing and squirting water. The best part was when Auntie B. slipped and slid all the way down the muddy bank on her bottom. I was snorting and laughing so hard I thought my trunk would fall off! So was everybody else! Even Winston, with his big white tusks, couldn't help laughing.

Grandmama told me that I should feel very special because Winston does not attend the birthday of all young Elephants. Now that he's on the Bull Council, Winston has many duties and is always busy.

Everyone looks up to him, but at the party, you wouldn't know that he was such a famous and serious Bull. Winston was laughing and squirting water just like the rest of us! He even challenged me to a trunk wrestling match and I won! Well, to be honest, everyone knew he was pretending to lose so I could win on my birthday. But it was fun anyway.

I ate so many pods that I looked like one! We didn't leave the river until the sun started to set. And to top it off, on our way back we pushed through acacia bushes. I don't think anything feels better than branches and thorns scratching my back! It was a perfect day.

I wish you'd been there. We all trumpeted a birthday cheer for you. Did you celebrate at the zoo? I hope the keepers did something special. It makes me sad to think that you are alone, without your family, on your birthday. Oh, I just remembered! I saved you some pods. I'll keep them safe under my grass pillow until you get here. Okay, I have to go to sleep now. I can't keep my eyes open any longer!

Birthday Trumpets from
Your Cousin,
Kani

The young African Elephant folded the letter he had just written, slid it into an envelope and sealed it shut with his trunk tip. After tucking the letter under his sweet grass pillow, Kani lay down and in a few moments fell fast asleep. The moon shone and starlight showered down upon the tired young Bull who was happily dreaming of pods and mudbaths.

While Kani lay sleeping under African skies, his cousin Billy was just waking up thousands of miles away.

It was a day like any other day at the zoo until Billy spied the birthday letter from Kani. Grabbing the envelope, he opened it excitedly, eager to hear news from Kenya. Billy read the letter twice over and after finishing, sat down to write back.

Dear Kani,

Happy birthday to us, Cousin! It was great hearing from you! The river party sounded awesome! Wow! You really trunk wrestled with Winston? I bet all the other young Bulls were jealous!

We didn't do anything here for my birthday. In fact, I forgot it was our birthday, so thanks for reminding me. The zoo doesn't celebrate birthdays unless a new baby Animal is born. But when that happens, all the television and news people come and take pictures and there are balloons and bands and good snacks!

We've been pretty busy here too. The biggest news is that we're getting a new Elephant exhibit. That's what they call our room here. It's still made of concrete and bars but we'll have a pond! Even Lucy is excited. You remember Lucy, the Elephant Auntie who adopted me here? She says it's the first time that the zoo has done anything new to the exhibit.

We've had to live in a small stall while the building is going on. That part's not much fun because we have even less space!

I overheard one of the workmen say that it was a good thing that I was locked up because I scared him. I guess I'm getting to be big Elephant after all! I wish the keepers wouldn't lock us up. I hate being stuck in this old concrete box with all the excitement going on. The workmen carry toolboxes that are filled with all sorts of fun things.

Lucy and I will have a lot more room. It probably doesn't sound like much compared with the African Savanna, but if you had to share a tiny space with another Elephant, you would know what I mean. It gets pretty crowded day after day and Lucy gets so grumpy when I bump into her. Maybe with all this new room, the keepers will bring in another Elephant. I hope it's another Bull so we can play together. Lucy is old enough to be my mother and doesn't like to do anything except stand in the corner.

Oh, there's some more news – we're getting a different trainer! Lucy is all upset and keeps swaying back and forth saying that it can only get worse. But I tell her: "How can he be worse than the last trainer?" Sometimes Lucy is just no fun at all. I wish she was more like the Aunties. I really miss Auntie B. and Auntie Vivi. They were always cheerful and took such good care of me when Ma was busy looking for shoots and roots. I remember falling asleep as Auntie Vivi rubbed my head with her trunk. And Angela! She was just like a big sister to me. I loved her smile. How is she?

Okay, I'm going to sign off now. Lucy is stuck against the wall bobbing her head up and down so I had better go cheer her up.

Sending a big high five trunk!
Your Cousin,
Billy

CHAPTER III

Danger In The Air

It was several months before Kani was able to write back to his cousin Billy. There had been a long drought in Kenya. The days of fresh grass and brimming waterholes were gone. The once bright and friendly sun had now become an enemy. There was no way to escape the heat. Some Animals began to perish from thirst. Everyone prayed for the rains that made life on the Savanna possible.

Dear Billy,

Nyota brought your letter today. Remember Nyota? Nyota's my second cousin with the double-V notch in his right ear. While he was bringing it over to me, he dropped and stepped on it. He's such a nice Bull, but sometimes he can be so clumsy! Anyway, even though the envelope got all dirty and smudged, I can still read the letter inside.

We've been having a rough time here. There was a terrible drought. It was as if the rain just disappeared. Some days the clouds stacked up like soft white mountains so we were sure that the rains were coming. But every time, we were disappointed. Not a drop of rain fell and the clouds melted away like the snow on Mt. Kilimanjaro on a summer's day.

Nothing stopped the heat. The ground got so hot it burned our feet. None of the Animals had enough food to eat or water to drink. Baby Gazelles just fell where they stood and then lay there, too weak to get up. Vultures filled the sky. It was very sad and scary.

It was even more scary to see Grandmama worry. Usually she's the one calming everyone down, telling us to be patient, that the rains will come and that we should just look after the babies. You know, she can be pretty strict, but she has to be! She's our Matriarch and has the responsibility of leading the Family. She's the one who steps in when the Aunties don't agree, and teaches everyone how to find the right grass and where the juiciest roots are hidden. Grandmama is so respected that the Big Bulls come to her for advice.

But underneath all those grey wrinkles and stern face, she's the nicest person you could ever meet. Grandmama shows me where to find the sweetest pods and I swear she was laughing the hardest when Auntie B. slid down the riverbank on my birthday! Of course, Grandmama tried to hide her smile behind her trunk, but she couldn't hide her HUGE body shaking with giggles!

That's why we all began to feel very nervous. It wasn't like Grandmama at all to get up and pace at night. Every morning she was up before everyone else.

Every dawn, just as the sun peeked over the trees, Grandmama (or Nobantu, as the Bulls and Aunties call her) would walk to the top of the hill. There she would stand very still and lift her trunk to sniff the air.

We watched her hold her head just so, listening for thunder and looking for a flash of lightening – any sign that said rain was on its way. But day after day, week after week, month after month nothing happened. Then one day the rains came! Oh, Billy, to feel the rain shower over us!

We were so happy. Everyone was trumpeting, chirping, and snorting! The lakes filled so high that when the Lions came to drink their bellies touched the water. The Kudus, Wildebeest, Storks, and Buffalos splashed around just like kids! At last, all of us were able to relax. We were having a wonderful time. But that didn't last for long.

All of a sudden, everyone stopped what they were doing. Gazelles stopped eating. Birds stopped singing and Baboons stopped teasing each other. No one moved. We stood still listening. Then, we heard it. There it was, a growl that got louder and louder. It was a flood! A flood was coming!

All the Animals began to run. Zebras galloped by as if chased by Lions. Storks flew off in all directions squawking and Giraffes loped past with their long necks swaying in the wind. All the Animals moved so fast there was almost a stampede!

Grandmama raised her trunk high and trumpeted for us to follow. Mothers and Aunties ran to gather the Babies. Winston and the other Bulls charged over to help lead the Families to safety.

The rain that had been a gentle friend now bit into our skin, stinging and mean. Tiny creeks became big brown rivers in just a few seconds. The water that had tasted so sweet turned angry and grabbed at our feet as we struggled. Two Zebras were swept away before they could get to land. When we reached the shore, we ran as fast as we could up the slope, but the dry earth had turned to mud and our feet slipped and slid.

Finally, we made it to safety. Grandmama told us to make a circle around the babies. They were crying and looked so small. It was terrible, but we had all made it.

The next day, the sun came out. There was not a cloud in the sky. Birds were singing and new shoots and flowers burst out everywhere. It was as if nothing had happened. I learned an important lesson from the Big Flood. Good things can suddenly turn bad and bad things can suddenly turn good.

I'm going to get some sleep now. We haven't gotten much rest. Write soon. I haven't heard from you in a while. Maybe your letters got lost in the flood.

Your Cousin,
Kani

CHAPTER IV

Remembering

Dear Kani,

Lucy and I were so relieved to finally hear from you. But we were upset that you and the Family were in such danger. Thank goodness you are now safe. I did not know that the rains could be so dangerous! Here, when rain comes, we zoo Animals are happy. The Parrots sing, Henry Lion and Jonny Jaguar give out roars – and even Lucy and I let out a trumpet! The sidewalks get wet, the rain drums on the metal roof, and the air becomes fresh and clean. The sweet smell of rain is such a nice change from city smoke and smog.

But, I now understand how rain in the African Savanna is different. It gives life but can also take life away. Grandmama is truly a great Elephant Matriarch, and Winston – well, there isn't a finer Bull in all of Kenya!

I don't have any good or bad news to report. No scary flood or happy rain. It's the same old routine here day in and day out.

Hay in the morning, hay at noon, hay at night, and bananas when the zoo visitors come. Even the weather stays the same.

Well, there is a little news. By the time you get this letter, Lucy and I will be living in the new exhibit. The workmen painted the cement walls green and brown to look like an African forest. Humans are funny. Do they really think that Lucy and I will think that painted walls are real trees? The zoo must think that we Elephants are that stupid.

The new room is great, but isn't as big as I thought it would be. The pond is made of cement and is so small I can barely

stand in it. Someone threw in a big red ball and an old log. That's it. Nothing else. No acacia trees, no tall green grass, and no sparkling water like home! And there is no one but Lucy and me so it feels really lonely. It sure would be nice to have a couple of Ground Hornbills for company. . . Hey, remember how we used to chase them back home and Ma would get so mad? "Imenti," she'd scold, "How would you like to be chased by someone twenty times your size? Your Father would be ashamed at you picking on someone so small. Besides, you never know when you might need the Hornbills for friends. They always let us know when there is danger." (That's funny! I haven't thought about my old, real name, Imenti, in a while. I like my zoo name, Billy, much better.)

Yes, Ma was right. It wasn't very nice teasing that old bird, but it sure was fun!! Do you remember Mother Hornbill? She was tough. There was more than once when I thought she would get me with her lo-o-n-n-ng black beak. But, you know, Ma was wrong about one thing. The Hornbills didn't let us know when there was danger. Where were they when the helicopters came?

Billy stopped writing and looked up, staring into space. Time evaporated and he was no longer at the zoo but far, far away, years before, to the day when he was a two-year old walking through the African Savanna with his mother and the Elephant Family. Billy remembered it as if it had happened yesterday.

The sun had felt warm on his back and the air was fragrant with sweet grass. Everyone in the Family was relaxed and peaceful. Kani, Benjamin, Little Beth, the Aunties, and Billy were having fun playing in the long grass. Then, out of the blue, the sky began to buzz with the sound of angry Bees. The buzz got louder and louder.

At once, the world exploded. It wasn't Bees at all. They were Humans with guns in shiny metal helicopters who had come to kill the Elephants!

Bullets rained down on the Family. Mothers and Aunties cried out and tried to shelter the young Elephants with their bodies. Billy called to his mother but before he could reach her, she fell before his eyes. Guns continued to fire and more Elephants fell to the ground. The air filled with smoke and noise. Billy ran toward the forest confused and terrified. He heard his cousin Kani calling to him:

"Cousin, Cousin! Come this way! Come this way! Imenti!" Billy turned toward his cousin's voice, but just as he got to the safety of the forest edge, Billy felt big powerful hands grabbing and tearing at him. He tried to struggle free but the men were too fast. They tied the baby Elephant's legs with ropes and tethered him to the body of a fallen Auntie. Billy could hear other young, captured Elephants crying.

When the shooting stopped, the men rounded up all the baby Elephants. Billy was shoved into the back of an old smelly truck. The truck gate slammed with a Bang!

Try as he might to see his Mother for the last time, Billy could not. He was too small to see over the wooden sideboards. The truck engine turned over and started down the red dusty track. Billy shrank into a corner, crying and trembling. His Mother was gone, his Family was gone, and life on the Savanna was over forever.

Zoo noises broke through Billy's dream of the past. Henry Lion roared and Billy woke, startled. Memories of the Savanna vanished and were replaced by cold concrete walls. The young Elephant looked over his shoulder and saw Lucy. As always, she stood silently swaying in her corner. The red ball sat motionless by the edge of the pond. After a few minutes, Billy sat up, straightened his shoulders and continued writing to his cousin.

I'm sure the Ground Hornbills could have heard the helicopter blades whirring long before we did. It makes me mad that the Hornbills weren't around to warn us about the men. If they had, then we could have gotten away and I wouldn't be stuck in this place so far from home. And Ma, well, Ma would still be alive with us. I guess it wasn't the Hornbills' fault, really. Oh well, I don't want to think about it. I have to go now, the banana bell rang and that means there will be a class of kids coming to visit the zoo. Maybe they'll give us some peanuts too!

A big trunk hug from
Your Cousin,
Billy

Billy signed and folded the letter. After placing it on the ground by the gate, he sadly turned away. There hadn't been a banana bell after all. He just didn't want his tears to fall on the letter. Then Kani would have known he had been crying and Billy couldn't let that happen. After all, Billy thought, he was supposed to be a grown up Bull by now and big Bulls don't cry. He walked over and kicked the red ball. He watched it roll over to the chain link fence and bounce back until it rested against the other wall. The world felt very small and empty.

CHAPTER V

Peace On the Plain

After the flood, life on the Savanna settled into its peaceful rhythm. The Wildebeest Migration pulsed through the Serengeti and the Elephants began their travels along the Ancient Path. Once more, Kani and his young friends were able to play with carefree joy. However, while the frightening waters may have receded, the shadow of a new danger threatened.

Dear Billy,

Greetings from Kenya! Things are much better since I last wrote. The drought is finally over and so is the Big Flood! Everyone is relaxed and we can go about life without worrying. All the water and sweet grass have made everyone happy.

These days have been really nice. We've all been down by the waterhole – the one where you and I got into so much trouble for splashing Edwin! You would hardly recognize him. Back then he was just a teenager like us now. Today, he is almost as big a Bull as Winston!

No one has time to bother each other because there's so much good food! The Lions and Hyenas have been hanging out with the Zebras, Gazelles, and Wart Hogs like old friends!

Grandmama is trying to decide if we should move on and join some of the other Families for a while. There's still lots of grass and water, but she's heard news with her feet that ivory poachers have been seen around the park.

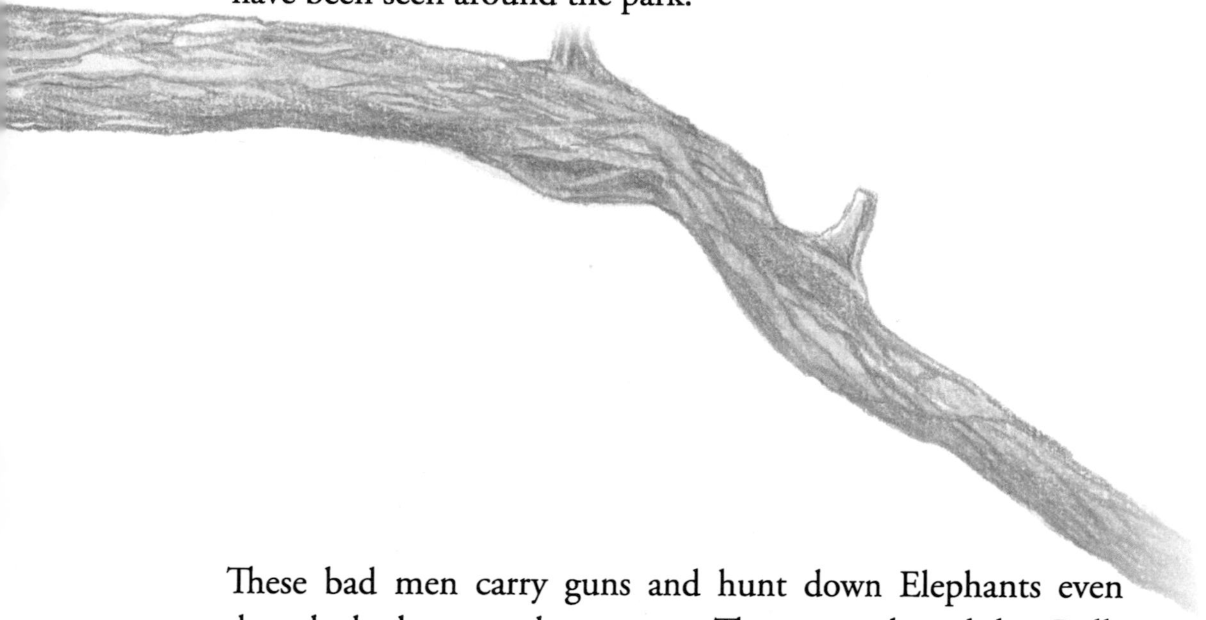

These bad men carry guns and hunt down Elephants even though the law says they cannot. They try and catch big Bulls like Winston and even go after the Aunties and babies.

I wish we could stay here – the grass is so sweet and the water so tasty - but Grandmama thinks we need to move on. I must admit it's hard to have fun when you feel like a poacher might show up any minute. . . I will let you know what Grandmama decides to do and send a message about where we are headed on the Path.

Everyone waves a trunk hello and Grandmama told me to tell you to come home soon. We all miss you.

– Your Cousin,
Kani

CHAPTER VI

Monkey Business

Back at the zoo, half way 'round the world and far from the worries of poachers and hunters, Billy and his zoo friends had other things on their minds.

Dear Kani,

Your letter made me so homesick for the Family. And all that talk about sweet grass makes my mouth water! I couldn't stop snorting and laughing when you reminded me of the trouble we got into sneaking up on Edwin and splashing him. I always wondered if he would play that same trick on us! I am sorry to hear that you and the Family have to move on because of the hunters. Elephants on the Savanna don't seem to be able to find a day of peace anymore.

Not like here. There's nothing but boring peace here! It's true that with the new space I almost have enough room to run a little! But Lucy hasn't changed.

At first, when we were let into the new exhibit, she seemed kind of excited, but that didn't last long. She's gone back to her old sad ways, swaying back and forth and back and forth or just stands there with her forehead pressed against the wall. I don't think she was always this grumpy and unhappy. It must be because of all the time she's spent alone here in the zoo. She's lived in this old concrete box for over thirty years. Hey, I just remembered some real news!

Last week, when the keepers were cleaning out cages before the zoo opens for the visitors, the head keeper, Will, started yelling and carrying on: "Jo Jo's out, Jo Jo's escaped!" Jo Jo's the Chimpanzee who lives three exhibits down from us. He's been here almost as long as Lucy. Jo Jo's a nice old fellow. He likes to tease and play jokes and has always got a smile for everybody.

Anyway, right after Will started up, everyone chimed in. Henry Lion and Jonny Jaguar started roaring, the Monkeys in the Monkey House jumped up and down and threw fruit and rocks, the pink Cockatoos called out all sorts of things, and Parker Peacock fanned his feathers like playing cards! Well, what's new?! Parker does that at the drop of a hat. Any chance he can get – whoosh – there goes his tail! What a show off!

Then the real fun began. Sirens blared and policemen jumped out of their cars and ran toward the zoo. The keepers used loudspeakers telling everyone to watch out: “Alert! Alert! Jo Jo’s out!” It was kind of funny, but after a while it seemed kind of stupid. I mean what can an old chimp do? He’s not mean and wouldn’t hurt anyone. But these Humans in blue suits with guns and clubs rushed through the zoo entrance all upset. One of them got stuck in the turnstile and it took three people to get him out!

I was laughing so hard that I didn’t realize how much noise I was making until the new trainer came over and poked me with the ankus. An ankus is a nasty pointed steel stick that the trainer uses to make us do things. That got me mad. I wasn’t doing anything wrong, just watching like everyone else. And he didn’t have to use that thing. It really hurt. Lucy and I both have scars from the ankus.

The keepers don’t seem to realize that if they would just ask us nicely or be a little patient, we’d go along sweet as rain. They should know that Elephants are polite and considerate.

Back to Jo Jo. The chase took hours. They searched high and low for the old Chimpanzee but no one could find him. Somehow he had managed to pry open his cage latch and climb out. It was almost noon before they finally caught him. Someone

yelled: "There he is!" After that, I didn't see much because the keepers had locked me up in the back stall. Later, when they let me back out, Lucy told me that Jo Jo hadn't run away after all. He escaped from his cage but after running around for a while dodging the keepers and police, the old Chimpanzee decided the fun was up and went back inside. When the keepers caught up with him, Jo Jo had snuck back into his cage. And there he was, sitting behind the fake tree where he has a little hidey hole, munching on some caramel corn that he'd picked up outside on the sidewalk.

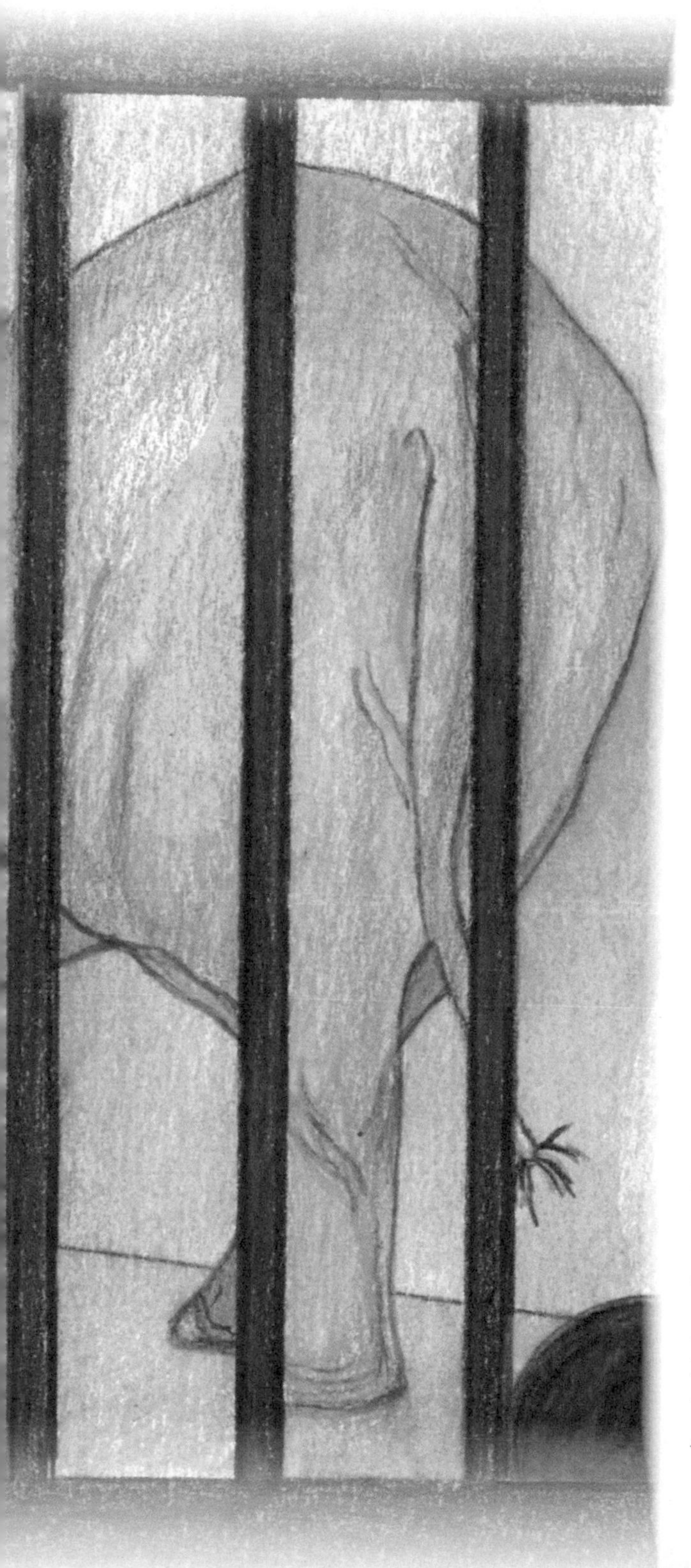

Kani, you know, it's funny. I was wondering why didn't Jo Jo escape when he had the chance? He could have been gone in a flash. But he didn't. He just went right back to that dirty old cage. Lucy says that when you stay in the zoo long enough, even if you hate it, it's still the only place you know. There's nowhere else to go and no family anymore. The zoo is the only home you have. Well, not for me. I'm headed back home to Africa as soon as I can!

It's been pretty quiet ever since. I think everyone felt a little disappointed that Jo Jo didn't get away. The keepers haven't let him out of his backroom. They locked him up out of sight from visitors and there's a sign that says "Chimpanzee Exhibit Temporarily Closed." Seems like they're punishing Jo Jo or maybe he just doesn't feel well. I saw the doctor give him a shot in his arm with a big needle.

Okay, I have to sign off now. Lucy's calling and looks scared. She's started to do that a lot these days. All of a sudden she panics. She won't stop crying and bobbing until I come over and put my trunk around her neck. I tell her stories of Africa and that seems to make her feel safe again.

Drop a trumpet on the trunkline to let me know you and the Aunties and Grandmama are well.

High five trunking,
Billy

CHAPTER VII

A Sad Day

It was again many months before Billy heard back from his cousin Kani. Billy lived in a fog of forgetfulness. The young Elephant often stood for hours on end without moving. If it wasn't for the occasional twitch and curl of his trunk tip you would have thought he was a statue. Some days Lucy and Billy never even spoke a word to each other. Both were lost in their memories, worlds away from the zoo.

Almost an entire year had passed. There was still no word from Kani. Billy's impatience turned to worry. It wasn't like his cousin to be so quiet for so long. "I'm going to write him," Billy said firmly, "I'm going to write Kani again in case the other letters got lost. Maybe this one will get through." Billy walked over to the exhibit corner and sat down to write.

Dear Kani,

I haven't heard from you in such a long time. Maybe the letters got lost. . . I am thinking of you. Send news as soon as you can.

Your Cousin,
Billy

The young Elephant folded the letter and slid it carefully into the white envelope. Using the tip of his trunk, Billy sealed the envelope shut. After the letter was sent, Billy waited anxiously for news. More days passed. Still no word from Kenya. Then, finally, a letter arrived! Billy trumpeted with joy and tore open the envelope eager to hear about Kani's exciting adventures and news of the Family. But his smile quickly vanished when he read the first sentence.

Dear Billy,

Winston is dead. Ivory poachers. Everyone's crying. I can't write more. The Family is on the run, hiding. I will write as soon as I can.

Your Cousin,
Kani

Billy froze, shocked by the news. In an instant, the young Elephant was flung back to the day of the cull when his mother was killed. He smelled the smoke and heard the gunfire. Billy called out, "Ma! Ma!" and saw her fall before his eyes.

Billy's screams broke through Lucy's dream world. She turned from the wall and lumbered over to the young Elephant as quickly as her aching old body would allow. "Billy!" she cried, "Billy, it's all right, it's me, Lucy! You're with me!" Lucy reached out and caressed his face with her trunk, desperately trying to wake the young Elephant from his nightmare. But Billy would not, could not, stop sobbing. He struggled free and ran to the other side of the exhibit where he picked up the old log and tossed it high into the air. "My name is Imenti! My name is Imenti!" he bellowed.

The commotion brought the keepers running. But instead of calming Billy, they grabbed a fire hose hanging outside the exhibit. The two men stood firm, readying for the hose's powerful blast. They turned it on the frightened young Elephant. The spray was so strong that it pushed Billy up against the wall. Water filled Billy's trunk so that he could hardly breathe. He choked and coughed.

Lucy lunged forward, pushing herself between the cold blast of water and the young Elephant now driven to his knees. Turning to face the exhibit front, Lucy angrily confronted the two keepers. Magnificent in her defiance, Lucy stood her ground, once again the regal African Matriarch whom she was born to be. With a mighty roar, she raised her trunk in warning, and commanded the keepers to STOP!

Wisely, the keepers quickly took heed. They turned off the water, and in their panicked haste to get away from the towering Elephant Matriarch fell on their backsides and scrambled away, never taking their eyes off Billy's protector.

Lucy and Billy were left alone. Water stood in pools on the concrete floor. The other zoo Animals were silent and the only sound to be heard was the soft hum of highway traffic rushing by. Lucy gently helped Billy to his feet. Folding her trunk around his shoulders like a comforting blanket, she walked by his side until they reached the back corner. There, Lucy tucked Billy in for the night. She never left his side.

Early the next morning, Billy wrote his cousin. His trunk shook and his body still stung from the needle sharp spray of the fire hose.

Dear Kani,

I can't believe that Winston is dead. He was one of the toughest and smartest of all Bulls. How could this have happened? Is everyone else okay? Did the Family move on? Grandmama and the Aunties must be heartbroken.

With great sadness from
Your Cousin,
Billy

CHAPTER VIII

Saying Good-Bye

Dear Billy,

Sorry I haven't written in so long. We've all been in shock. It still does not feel real. After Winston was killed, Grandmama took us on walkabout. We had to go. The danger from the poachers was too great. It's even unsafe where we are now. The Family has to hide in the forest during the day and wait until night before we venture out to find food and water.

The day Winston died was the worst day of my life. It was as bad as when the men took you away. The day had started off so beautifully! There we were, having a nice quiet morning browsing sweet grass and scratching our backs on acacia thorns. Everyone was feeling just grand when all of a sudden Edo came running and screaming. He was so upset, we couldn't understand what he was saying.

Grandmama charged up and put her trunk around Edo's neck telling him to calm down and speak slowly. Then we heard. "It's Winston! It's Winston! They've shot Winston! Winston is dead!"

Edo said that ivory poachers snuck into the park and shot Winston with their big guns. No one is allowed to hunt in the park, but somehow these men got in at night. Winston was the first to spot them. With a mighty roar that shook the trees, he charged straight toward the men to protect the other Elephants. The poachers started shooting but that didn't stop Winston. He kept charging right into the blaze of guns. But the bullets were too many and the guns too powerful and Winston finally collapsed to the ground. Before he died, the gunmen set upon him, took out their big knives and cut off his tusks.

We couldn't go right away, but as soon as she thought it was safe enough, Grandmama took the Family to say goodbye to Winston. She told us that we would come back every year to visit his bones like we do with the other Family who have passed on. One by one we went up and spoke to him with our trunks. I had never touched someone who had gone home. "Gone home" – that's what Grandmama says dead really means because being here on the Savanna is really just a visit from our real home, the place where all Elephants, all the Ancestors, all the Great Bulls and Matriarchs, go and live after they die.

Mama says touching someone who has gone home is really listening and that when you get older and touch someone like Winston, you can hear him speak. "It's like singing," she says, "When you touch the Ancestor's bones you can hear their voices. The songs come from old white bones." When I went up to Winston, I was a little scared. Even though he was a wise, kind Bull, Winston was always a bit intimidating. Suddenly, there he was, lying on the ground, all quiet. I wanted to hear Winston's voice again. I wanted him to sit up and laugh in that way that he did and say in his deep rich voice: "Ha, Little Kani, I was just fooling you!" But he didn't. He just lay there cold and silent. When I touched his face, I tried to hear the singing but I couldn't hear anything. Mama said not to worry because when I become initiated into the big Bull group, I will learn how to listen – to hear and sing with the Ancestors.

After we all had said good-bye to Winston, we gathered round Grandmama. She told us that Winston was one of the biggest and noblest of Bulls. He had just started going into musth. He was a real grown-up Bull. All the girls had a crush on him. They were always trying to catch his attention. But he pretty much ignored them and hung out with the other Bulls. I know he was one of Grandmama's favorites. We all miss Winston terribly.

To tell you the truth, Cousin, I am starting to get nervous. I heard Mama and Grandmama whispering together. They were talking about how I need to leave the Family and join the Big Bull group. They said it is high time that I start studying with the Bulls. It'll be great not having to tell my mother everything, where I'm going, who I'm going with, and what I'm eating. But at the same time, the Bulls are kind of a tough crowd. . .

Billy, I wish there was something you and I could do. The Elders have told us how millions of Elephants have been killed and their families destroyed for their ivory tusks. But until Winston was murdered, I didn't believe this could be true. How can Humans be so cruel? How could anyone do that to someone like Winston? Do you think you could talk to the Humans you meet and tell them what happened to Winston? Do you think they could tell other Humans to stop? Maybe if people knew how Elephants suffered, they wouldn't think ivory was so beautiful anymore. Maybe if they realized that Elephants are people too, then they would stop hurting us and the other Animals. . . But those people at the zoo - you say that they like Elephants, yet they are the ones who keep you and Lucy locked up!

Come home, Cousin. We need you here. Something has to be done now because they're going to keep on killing until none of us are left.

With a heavy heart,
Your Cousin
Kani

CHAPTER IX

Song of the Savanna

Dear Kani,

Your letter arrived today. I am glad everyone else is safe. Lucy and I were so worried. But it sounds like you and all other Elephants are still in great danger. I am sad and angry that I am stuck here and cannot help. Life feels even more lonely and empty.

There is so much that I will never know about our great Elephant Society. Lucy tries to tell me what she knows. But she was captured and taken to a zoo when she was only a baby as well!

I didn't know about Elephants "going home" or even about listening and the singing Ancestors' bones. When I get back to Africa, you'll have to bring me to where Winston died – I mean, where he went home. Then you and I and some of the other Bulls can go after and catch those ivory poachers!

I'm starting to hate Humans. Think I'll change my name back to Imenti. Using my real name makes me feel more at home – and more like an Elephant! It's hard to feel like an Elephant when you live in a zoo. Maybe the people here can help stop the poaching and hunting. You know, I have some influence. The keepers tell me that I am the most popular exhibit at the zoo! I get the most visitors of any Animal here and the children love me! I bet that if they knew what the poachers had done to Winston and how we are losing our homes, the children would get their parents to make it stop.

You know, Kani, Human children are a lot like us. They laugh and have fun with their families just like Elephants! If anyone can help us, the children can!

Send Elephant love to everyone from me and Lucy. Give a special big trunk hug to Grandmama. Tell her I'm trying to get home as fast as I can.

The young Bull signed his name "Billy," but then, he hesitated. After a moment, he slowly scratched out "Billy" with his pen and carefully wrote "Imenti" in its place.

In solidarity
Your cousin,
~~Billy~~
Imenti

When he finished writing his letter to Kani, Billy walked over to the back of the stall where a tiny corner of sky peeked through the roof. It made Billy happy to think that he and Kani were standing under the same sky. He stared up, straining and stretching his trunk as high as he could as if he might touch the night sky above. But try as he might, he couldn't see any stars. The city lights were too bright. Disappointed, Billy turned away. Suddenly, he heard something.

"What was that?" Billy thought. It didn't sound like anything he had ever heard before at the zoo. Was that music he heard? He leaned forward in the dark and listened more carefully. Yes! There it was! A distant melody came floating across the night air. He listened some more and now he could hear these chanted words:

"Sasa ni usiku, Mimi naona nyota! Sasa ni usiku, Mimi naona nyota!" The words sounded familiar to Billy but he could not quite place them. Then, suddenly, he remembered. "Sasa ni usiku, Mimi naona nyota!" Billy repeated, his face brightening with recognition, "Now is the night, I can see the stars!"

The chanting got louder and louder and then the singing began. First, there were the soft voices of the Gazelles. Then there came the lyrical notes of the Lark, followed by joyful Elephant trumpets. Lions, Hornbills, Zebras, and the other Animals took up the chorus. Soon all the Savanna and zoo Animals were singing.

Billy stood tall, his heart swelling, and he began to sing in a strong sweet voice. The walls of the zoo vanished and for a moment all Animals were joined together. Henry was back with the Lions in Africa, the Hornbills were with wild Hornbills, and Zebras, Kudus, Warthogs, and everyone else was reunited with their friends and families. The night sky filled with song and stars! Then gradually, the music softened and the Animals' voices dropped out one by one until only Billy remained singing to himself. The stars faded away and the exhibit walls closed in, but Billy kept singing softly, "Sasa ni usiku. Now it is night. Mimi naona nyota. I can see the stars! Sasa ni usiku, mimi naona nyota!"

As he closed his eyes to sleep for the night, Billy could still hear the music. In a few moments he was fast asleep, a smile on his face, dreaming of his African Savanna home.

CHAPTER X

Graduation

Savanna life was ever changing. The years passed by like white rainclouds gliding over the African plain. Before too long, Kani had transformed from a brash, mischievous boy–Elephant to a strong young Bull. He had now joined the All Bull Group to begin his life as an adult in Elephant society.

Hello, Hello Cousin!

You're looking at a brand new Bull! I've graduated to the All Bull Group! One day, I decided that I had had enough of girls and so I up and joined the Big Bulls. Well, that isn't exactly how it happened. Grandmama and Mama kind of pushed me out, but I was thinking of going anyway.

The first few nights were scary. I had never been on my own without the Aunties and Mama. But now, it feels great! I spent a whole day just doing what I wanted – wallowing in mud baths, eating pods, and goofing off. It gets a little lonely at night, but we Bulls are never far from each other because we're always in touch. I can hear where everyone is through my feet even when I can't see them. It's not quite true that I can do whatever I want. We have a lot to learn. The Big Bulls are teaching us younger ones the Ancient Ways and we're always on the move, checking in on the other Elephants as well our own Family. Bull life is fun, but busy and tough a lot of the time.

Anyway, I wanted to let you know the news. I'm ready to sleep. Today was a big day so I think I'll grab a bit of sweet grass and tuck in for the night. I wish you were here with us.

Write soon.
Your Cousin, Kani

Unlike the African Savanna, life at the zoo dragged on. Time stretched out like a long black mamba in the morning sun, each day like the one before. Todays blended into yesterdays, and tomorrows into todays with hardly any notice. Because nothing changed on the outside at the zoo, it was hard for Billy to see the changes in himself. But he was changing. He was no longer a youngster. Billy too was growing up.

Dear Cousin,

Everything has been pretty quiet since Jo Jo the Chimpanzee breakout. Why, that's funny! For a minute, I forgot that it happened years ago and isn't news at all! Well, it seems new because everyone still talks about it. There's not much else to talk about since there is nothing really new going on at the zoo.

The keepers sent the doctor to me again because of my leg. I think it is just a little cut, but they seem to think it is serious. I got it a while ago. Martin the new trainer was trying to get me to do something that I didn't want to do so I ended up falling down and cut my leg on the concrete pool. The cut got worse and I got in the habit of rubbing it to make it feel better. I do that a lot when I get nervous.

After a few weeks, the cut turned into a sore and didn't go away so the keepers gave me medicine. It tasted awful. They tried to hide it in the bananas and oranges but that didn't fool me. Since I wouldn't swallow the medicine they chained me up so I couldn't reach my leg until it healed. The keepers are so unfair! They treat me like it was my fault when it was really Martin's. If he hadn't prodded me with the ankus and hurt me so much, then I wouldn't have backed up and slipped and fallen and then I wouldn't have gotten hurt and wouldn't have to be chained up.

Why don't they chain up Martin? He's the dangerous one! Lucy was right. Martin is meaner than the old trainer, Will. The other day, he tried to get me to paint a picture. Can you believe that? Why would an Elephant do something unnatural like that? Winston would never do anything as silly as painting a picture or pushing a red ball! So I lost my temper and threw the paint. Well, that was the last straw for Martin and that was when he cut me with the ankus and I fell. I am just getting sick of all this zoo stuff. One day I'll show them: "Enough is enough" and push back. Lucy keeps telling me not to get mad and complains that I am getting testy. She should talk!! Oh well, I'll stop complaining. Be well.

A Grumble Rumble from
Your Cousin,
Imenti

Hey Kani,

Haven't heard from you in a while. Is everything okay? I hope so. What are you and the other Bulls up to? I bet you are doing lots of fun things and having great adventures!

We had snow this week so Lucy isn't feeling very well. She says her feet hurt even more when it gets cold. They're cracked all over from standing around in one place on hard concrete. I hope my feet don't get like that.

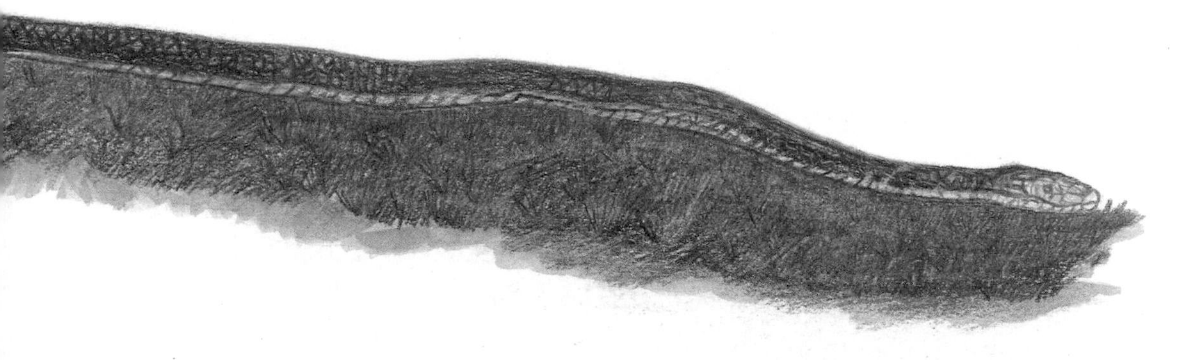

I'm planning on getting out of here as soon as I can and heading back to Africa to join you in the All Bull Group - and it may be sooner than later. The doctor and Martin were talking together the other day at Gina Giraffe's next door and I overheard them say that I was going to be moved soon. Wouldn't that be wonderful? Oh yeah! Some scientists came to study me and Lucy. I thought they might be smarter than the keepers. After all, they spend all their time studying Elephants. But listen to this. They told the keepers that Lucy and I need different kinds of food and things to play with to entertain ourselves. That all sounded good to me. But you know what they came up with?

A bunch of branches, shredded newspaper, some dry old pellets, and a recording of Elephant voices that included baby Elephants crying for their mothers! Lucy went crazy. She started looking for the babies in distress and started crying herself. Finally, the keepers got the message and turned it off. The food pellets tasted awful and got soggy by the pond. So that didn't work either.

All we are left with is a bunch of old sticks. As if sticks and walls painted to look like trees could ever replace our African home and Family. Gee, this letter is starting to ramble! Well, you get the picture.

Wish I could hear more often from you. Send me some exciting stories about you and the other Bulls. You all must be having a wild time out there on your own.

Your Boring Cousin,
Imenti

CHAPTER XI

The Ancient Path

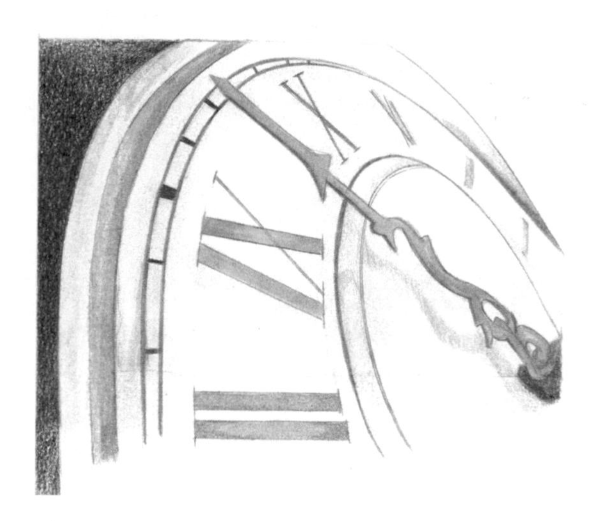

The wheel of time turned round and round and the lives of the two cousins became more and more separate. Kani lived free in the wild expanse of Africa, while Billy was confined to a tiny walled square in a zoo. But, despite the differences, the two cousins loved each other as much as ever.

Dear Imenti,

I can't believe so much time has passed since we last wrote. It is hard to believe that we are now both full grown Bulls, and not too young at that! Childhood seems very far away! We certainly had some fun then!

I have not been a very conscientious pen pal. The days here are difficult and our responsibilities as Big Bulls grow greater every day so there is little free time to write.

Yesterday, we returned from a long trek along the Ancient Path. Our journey was amazing! We were gone four months. Some days we walked over a hundred miles.

It depends on where we can get food and water. I had never been that far from home before, or rather I never knew our home was so big! Every night we watched the sun set but every day that same horizon was farther and farther away from where we started. We met all sorts of new Elephants. Some families, Matriarchs with the Aunties and babies tagging along with their little trunks. We also met groups of Bulls and those traveling alone.

I don't like to brag, but our Bulls were the biggest and strongest and had the longest tusks! I was so proud to be part of them. They are wonderful Bulls – loyal, smart, and will stick up for each other no matter what!

We were able to hear news from other parts of Africa and most news isn't good. Danger stalks our people everywhere. There are even more ivory hunters and Humans have taken more and more land so that there is nowhere Elephants can live in safety. The drought has made things worse. Food is very scarce.

Well, Cousin, I must stop writing now. Mishak and Edwin are calling me to Council. We have to decide where the Family can live with the most safety and what we must do to best escape the poachers. The rains are late, and the Matriarchs are worrying about the babies. Write me soon, I am ever

Your Cousin,
Kani

Dear Kani,

I got your letter about the trek along the Ancient Path! Just think – all that space to roam and all those stars you must have seen every night! It's hard for me to imagine how big the Savanna is and how many other Elephants there are!

It sure does sound like you and Mishak are busy with all that is happening with the Family and the herd. I guess your life in the Bull Council doesn't leave much time for writing. It's been so long since I got a letter from you, I almost stopped writing! At least the trunkline keeps me posted. . . But, today is our birthday so I just wanted you to know that I am thinking of you and sending happy pods and roots wishes.

Your Cousin,
Imenti

CHAPTER XII

A Time of Change

Dear Kani,

This time it's my turn to send some news! It's partly happy, partly sad news, though. First of all, Lucy is gone. I don't know if you remember me telling you about how sick she got. She could hardly stand, she had become so weak. Then one day, these people came and took her away in a big truck. They said she went to a place called Sanctuary.

After Lucy had been gone a couple of weeks, the zoo brought in a new Elephant named Barbara. She heard through the trunkline that Lesanju said that Hassan said that Jeffrey said that Lokesh said that Lucy went to a beautiful place where there are trees and waterholes and big barns for the Elephants when it gets cold. Even though it's kind of like a big zoo because you still live behind fences, the Sanctuary is much better. There are lots of other Elephants who can come and go as they please and everyone is really nice.

Lucy is doing much better. She's stronger and has gained weight. The Sanctuary soaks her aching feet in special herb baths. That makes me very happy, but I still feel bad. Lucy has always wanted to go back home to Africa and now it doesn't look like she ever will.

After Lucy left, I felt really lonely – so lonely that I even started talking to Parker Peacock! Talk about desperate! When Barbara first arrived, I thought I would have someone else to keep me company. But then, I found out she comes from Thailand and

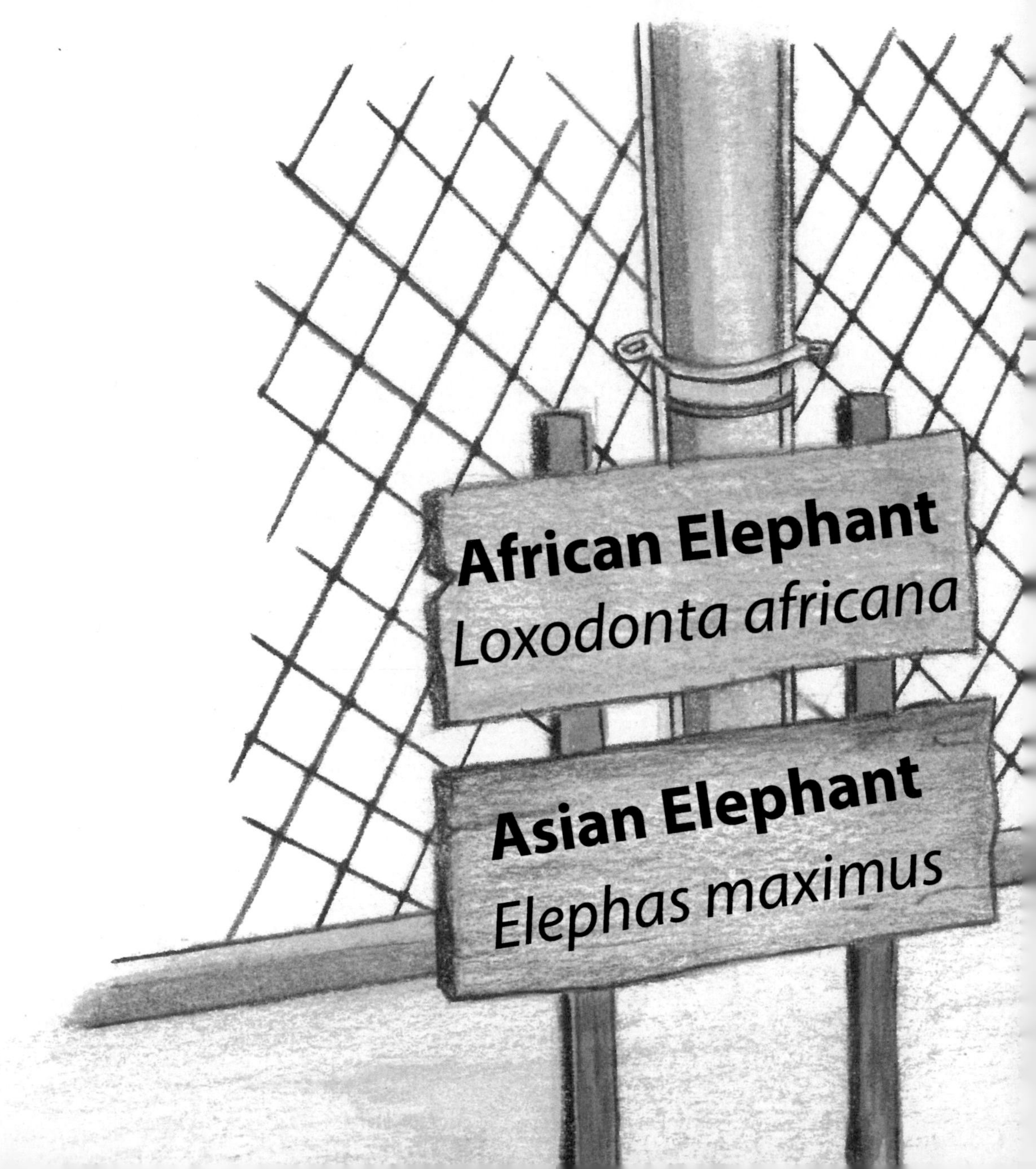

doesn't speak our dialect. Sometimes, I can't make trunks or tails of what she is trying to say. Plus she's just a kid, only thirteen. I don't know why they put her in with me, a grumpy old Bull from Africa. Most days, we stand on either side of the exhibit and don't talk. She gets depressed too and so we aren't much help for each other.

Jo Jo the Chimpanzee isn't doing too well. He tries to spend his time in his hidey-hole for privacy but the keepers lock it up so the visitors can see him.

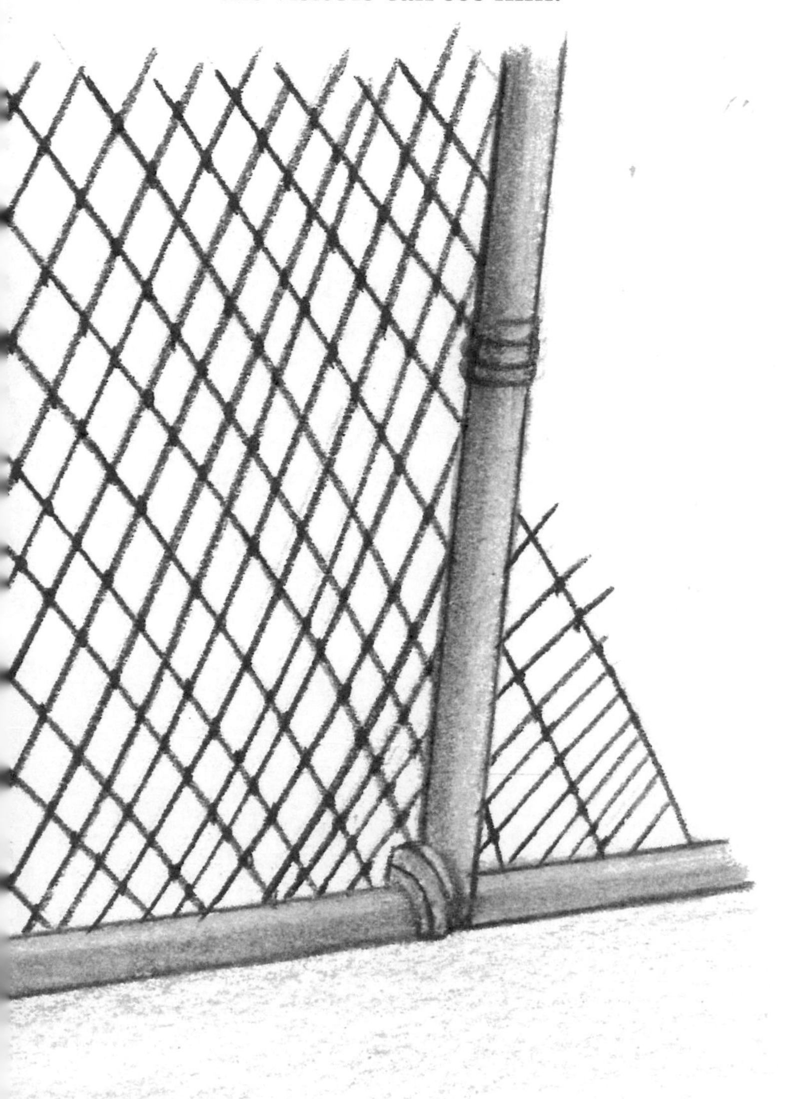

I think it makes him mad because he has started throwing things at people. He's gotten so thin and grey.

Tomorrow I'm supposed to learn a new trick from Martin. At least it'll be a change of scene. Write soon.

Your Cousin,
Imenti

Dear Kani,

Still haven't heard from you. But lately, I haven't been around either to get letters even if you had sent them. The keepers chain me up most of the time. I got angry one day and pushed Martin down and he broke his leg. Served him right. I mean who does he think he is shoving me around and treating me like a kid? I'm more than thirty some years old now, old enough to be considered a Big Bull. Plus my feet hurt and that puts me on edge. I'm getting sick of this place and ready to bust out. Keep your eyes peeled and get ready! I'm going to get out of here and home to Africa no matter what it takes!

Write soon. I need to know where to find you and the other Bulls when I get back.

Imenti

Billy angrily pushed the letter aside and looked up at the corner of sky straining to hear the Song of the Savanna once again. But there were no stars and there was no song. All he could hear was the lonesome roar of Henry Lion.

CHAPTER XIII

Humans Are Confusing

No matter how much time passed, Billy and Kani were never far from each other's thoughts. Kani was full grown, with long tusks, and a strong trunk. He had traveled far from the days of playful youth. He was a well-respected elder Bull, a great leader, revered by all Elephants. Kani's days were no longer carefree and he carried the many worries of the Elephants on his shoulders. Life on the Savanna was not easy. After thousands and thousands of years, Elephant life had changed.

Dear Imenti,

After another long journey, the Bulls and I have returned. I was not able to write before because we were on walkabout. Cousin, I am sad to tell you that home is not like it was in the Old Days.

In the past, there was the Ancient Path. Elephants traveled along its length generation after generation. The Ancient Path has kept us together. It has enabled us to survive droughts and floods.

There was hardly any place that Elephants did not live or travel. Now, life is changed. Our lands are cut into pieces. We are fenced inside tiny parks. There is so little room that some Elephants have begun to fight and kill each other. South of here, Bulls swell in rage and gore each other. As if that was not enough, there is other trouble.

So many Matriarchs have been killed that there is often no one to teach the young Aunties how to raise the young. I am ashamed to say that some mothers ignore their babies' cries. The poor little ones just stand there whimpering, frightened and no one cares. Human violence has spread to us like a disease. Elephants are starting to act like Humans.

Not all the Humans are bad, though. There is a woman here in Kenya who is as wise and kind as our Matriarch. She has the name of a flower, but we call her the Great Mother. Indeed, she is truly a Matriarch because she takes in and raises our lost and orphaned Elephant babies whose mothers have been slain.

For many years, the Great Mother has lived with the Elephants. She has learned the secrets that only Matriarchs know. Her knowledge is so vast that she is able to heal young Elephants so they can go back and live with our wild herds again. She, her family, and friends have saved many, many Elephants. In recognition of her friendship and service, we invited her into Elephant society where she is now an Honorary Elephant Matriarch. If only more Humans were like her!

There is distant thunder and the skies are dark, Imenti. Chaka, Mishak, and the other Bulls are joining me in Council. We are worried about our Matriarch, Nobantu, and the Family who have not been seen in many months. The earth is silent when we listen for them with our feet. We leave at dawn tomorrow to find them.

My thoughts and heart are with you, as always
Kani

Wiping a tear from his eye with his trunk tip, Billy sadly lay his cousin's letter on the ground. The news from Kani was not good. Home was not the same as when he was a child Elephant in Africa. Billy was changed too. He had aged and was now an elder Bull. But, unlike Kani, Billy lacked the health of free living Elephants.

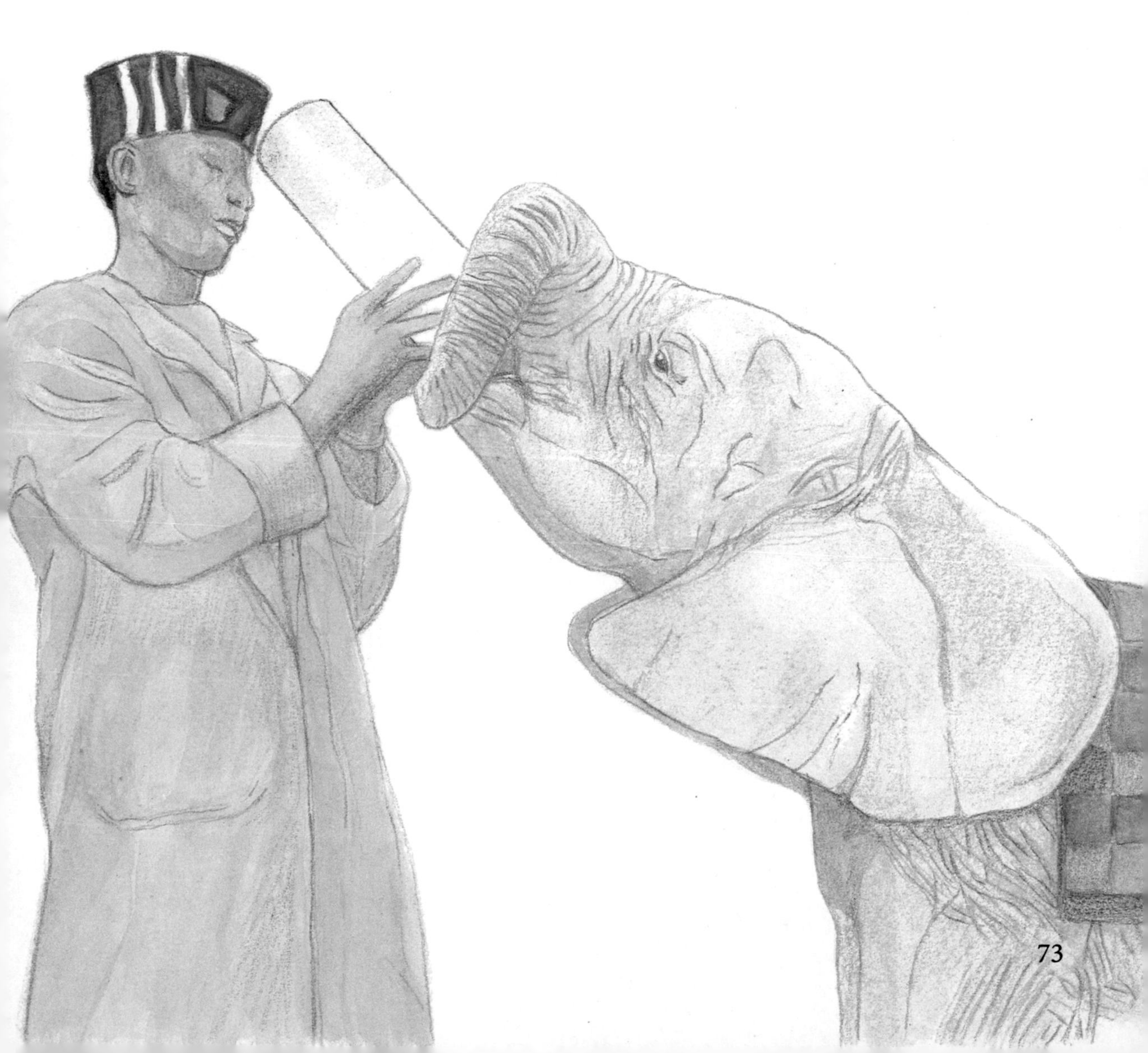

He was not able to walk the many miles that strengthen the legs and arms of a wild Elephant. There were no trees to pull down and uproot, which make Elephant trunks so nimble and strong. Billy's world was limited to the confines of four walls within a zoo exhibit and the only trees he saw were those painted on the concrete wall, faded and dirty after the many years.

Dear Kani,

I was so happy to hear from you after so long! But when I read your letter, I was very sad. I almost didn't recognize your voice, you sounded so different. Your voice reminds me of Winston. And now, you write, the Family is threatened.

It is difficult to believe so much has changed at Home. You say that there are many more Humans, and that they have become very violent and that we have lost much of the Old Lands. I didn't realize that life was so dangerous and that our people were starving. Now you say that Elephants fight among themselves. My heart weeps with this news.

Life at the zoo remains grey and cold. I live alone, you know. Barbara, the young Elephant from Thailand, wasn't much company, and anyway, they sent her to another zoo. There are

no other Elephants here. I heard one of the keepers talking about how they will "close the exhibit" when I die. I must say that wasn't very cheerful to hear! My feet hurt all the time and sometimes I have trouble breathing. But I always have enough energy to give Marty a kick. Marty is the nickname I gave the big red ball. I named it after Martin the mean trainer. Every time I kick the ball I think of him! It's a kick! Ha!

Not everyone's like Martin. We have some nice Humans here like your Great Mother. Take Ray, for instance. He's a good Human. He used to work in another zoo but quit when he realized how much we suffered in captivity. He did the best he could, but Ray could only help the zoo Elephants so much.

When he visits me, he sneaks in peanuts and watermelon and tells me stories. The rest of the time he stands there without talking, just to be with me. Ray is special. He listens to me. I talk to him and I know he understands.

At first, when Ray started coming to visit, I was afraid to get close with another Human, like I had in the past. A few years back, I tried to make friends with some scientists who came to see me. I thought we were friends but then one day, they just disappeared. After all the time I spent with them while they took measurements, they never even said good-bye. One day they just didn't show up. They never came back.

In the beginning, that made me scared. If one of our Elephant Family just ups and disappears, it's very bad news. It means that they have died or been injured in some way that prevented them from coming home. But Humans are not the same as Elephants.

Humans feel and do things differently than we Elephants. They don't seem to make friends for life like Elephants do. I asked Ray about this. Why, I asked him, do Humans want to put us in cages? Ray just shook his head and said he didn't know. But I think I know. I think it is because Humans live in zoos themselves – in places with artificial light where they can't even see the stars or feel the grass under their feet. I asked Ray about that too – why would anyone prefer to sleep on concrete rather than on the soft earth under the stars? He just smiled at me, sadly.

Okay, my dear Cousin, here I am rambling on and you have important things to do on the Bull Council. Be sure and write as soon as you hear news about the Family! Take care of yourself, too. Those poachers are dangerous.

Trumpets from Your Cousin,
Imenti

Dear Imenti,

Greetings, greetings! I can now send you good news from Africa! Yes, very good news indeed. We finally met up with Nobantu (Grandmama as you still call her), Auntie B, Angela, and the rest of the Family. The reason no one had seen or heard from them was because they were hiding in the forest to escape the ivory hunters. My Mother's injury has healed with herbs that Nobantu used. I may not have told you, but Mother was hurt badly.

We were out in the middle of a corn field when a villager threw a poison spear that lodged into Mother's side. We do not like to eat Human crops, but often there is no other food. Our land has been taken away and the drought has left nothing to eat. When the villagers saw us eating their crops, they became angry and tried to kill us. This is not fair. Elephants are respectful. They never take things away from other Animals and Humans. We are treated like trespassers when in truth we have lived on that land for thousands of years. We have always shared with others, but now we are considered pests.

How do they think we are to live? How are we to feed our children? And what kind of future can there be for Elephants with no food or land? These are the questions we ponder in Bull Council.

Finally, the Family was able to gather in a safe place. You should have heard all the trumpeting and seen all the trunk hugging! We have much to celebrate. Rain has come. This means that the grass will begin to green and so we can now move away from the Humans to a place where there is nourishment and water. And to top it all off, none of the Family had been harmed. Mother's wound was almost completely healed and Nobantu is as strong and strict as ever! The babies have started to smile again and wave their little trunks! It's enough to make even an old grumpy Bull like me smile!

Now to you, dear Cousin. Your last letter sounded very sad. It weighs heavily on my heart to hear that you are alone. Elephants do not do well without friends or family. Your keepers must be very cruel. But take heart, Cousin. The Family are forever at your side in spirit and love.

I must return to Council. Mishak is calling to me. There are new young Bulls to initiate and we must make plans to safeguard the Families. Our trunks reach out to you.

Your Cousin,
Kani

Big changes for Billy were also afoot. Like Kani, Billy was facing a new way of life – one with its own challenges.

Dear Kani,

I am overjoyed to receive news about you and the Family. I worry for you all. Savanna life, that once seemed to have the peace of paradise, has become so dangerous. Perhaps my own news will bring you some cheer – I am moving to Sanctuary! I am so excited, but also a little nervous because I'm not sure what to expect. Everyone says that Lucy is doing very well. Still, it's a big change for me. I wonder if I will turn out like Jo Jo the old Chimpanzee who lived so long in the zoo, he couldn't survive anywhere else. Remember? Even when he had the chance to escape, he came right back.

My friend Ray will be coming with me. He always promised that he would get me out, and so he did! He is a true Elephant friend! I shall have a different address, but that should be no problem as our trunkline makes sure we will always stay in touch. Nevertheless, I will be sure and write when I arrive.

Wish me luck, Cousin! Maybe after Sanctuary I can start planning my return to Africa. That will be the next step! Send the Family many strong trunk hugs.

Excitedly,
Your cousin,
Imenti

CHAPTER XIV

Letter from America

By the time Umkhulu had reached the last letters at the bottom of the brown parcel, the night sky had begun to show traces of the coming day. All the young Elephants remained huddled, listening intently, in a circle around the Old Bull's feet. They noticed that the Old Bull hesitated before taking out the last letter from the brown parcel. But, finally, he drew it out. The envelope looked different than all the others. This one was bigger, whiter, and newer. Slowly, the Old Bull laid the sheaf of pages on the ground and pushed them flat with his trunk tip. Taking a deep breath, Umkhulu continued to read.

Dear Mr. Kani,

Shikamoo! Greetings of respect! My name is Reggie, and I am the director of the Sanctuary where we rescue Elephants, like your cousin Billy, from zoos and circuses.

It is a great honor to write you. Billy spoke of you with such admiration and warmth. He told us about your Family and the adventures you shared as young Elephants in Kenya.

He proudly told us that you are a Great Bull, an Elder who leads the Council. Billy's African Family has become as familiar to us as our own mothers, fathers, aunts, brothers and sisters.

However, I write with great sadness that your beloved friend Billy has passed, or Gone Home, as he said is the correct way to talk about an Elephant's death. Billy had not received any letters from you for many years. At times, he shared his worry for you and the Family. He feared that harm might have come to you because life is now so dangerous for wild Elephants. But he always reassured himself, and us, that this was unlikely given what a brave Bull and brilliant Leader you are.

We breathed a great sigh of relief when Sabu, another Elephant, shared the news that you were well and thriving. I will never cease to be amazed by the Elephant trunkline, a communication network that crosses oceans, scales any zoo wall and bypasses circus chains! When I asked Sabu how she knew you were well – Sabu having spent the last twenty five years in a zoo – she answered with what I have learned is the usual Elephant answer: "The trunkline, of course! Jill told Helen who told Lokesh who told Nicky who told Ajok who heard from Dika who told Aitong who told me." The news is several months old now but we have faith that the Family remains in good health.

I wanted to tell you a little about your cousin's passing. Billy had many health problems from his long hard life in captivity. The years took their toll. But, after spending a few months here in Sanctuary, he recovered much of his strength. It is true that his feet were very damaged and that his body ached with arthritis. Nonetheless, he never lost his inner joy and sense of humor! Billy still liked to tease and tell stories. Everyone loved him so much! There was no kinder and wiser Elephant.

The change came in autumn as the leaves turned from green to red. Billy began to slow down and his eyes seemed to sparkle a little less. Then, one day, he walked up the hill to the big oak tree that he liked to sit under. When it started to get dark, Helen thought Billy might be getting cold so she trumpeted over to ask if he was okay. Billy liked to stay inside the barns on the colder nights as his arthritis was very painful and the crisp fall made it worse. Aitong offered to bring him some melon. (Watermelon was one of Billy's favorite treats!) But, your cousin said, "No, thank you! I'm doing grand. It's such a lovely sunset, I think I'll stay out a little longer. This clear sky promises some mighty fine stars!" That was the thing he loved best – gazing up at the stars.

Billy said when he looked up at the stars, he could imagine he was back in Africa with his cousin Kani listening to cicadas singing and the lions roaring. So we let him be and called out good night.

The next day, when we Human Carers rose and went out to breakfast with the Elephants, there was no one in sight. None of the Elephants could be seen, but it didn't take long to discover where everyone was. All the Elephants were gathered near the oak tree where Billy had sat the evening before. And there he was, only now he lay on his side.

Some of the Elephants were swaying and weeping. Billy's death, though peaceful, upset Helen and Lucy, in particular. Even though it has been many years since they left the zoo, Helen and Lucy still sway when they get anxious or upset. They say it helped them deal with the emptiness and fear of captivity. It was the only way they could escape, if only in their minds.

Other Elephants stood still facing Billy, their heads bowed. Then, one by one they each came up to him and touched his face and body with their trunks, as if listening or waiting for Billy to speak. We stayed there many hours together. It was a beautiful morning, like the ones when Billy trumpeted loudly upon waking. He loved life and showed it at every chance!

The Elephants asked us to let Billy lay where he was for a week. We did, although Human laws say you are not supposed to. At last, after many, many good-byes, we buried Billy under the oak tree. His passing has left a huge hole in our community. Lucy, of course, as Billy's adoptive Aunt, is very sad. People are still writing letters and sending flowers and watermelons that we bring to his grave.

I want you to know that you were in his mind and heart during his last hours, Mr. Kani. Indeed, he never forgot about you. He loved and admired you so very much. There is something else.

Although Billy finally stopped sending letters, he did write a last one to you and I enclose it here. I think you will find he finally found a home and peace here in Sanctuary after his terrible time at the zoo. We are comforted knowing that we were able to give to Billy something in return for the generosity that he showed to everyone he met. He was the kindest person I have ever known.

Our warmest wishes to You and The Elephant Family.

Sincerely,
Reggie from The Sanctuary

CHAPTER XV

Going Home

The Old Bull opened the second letter that the Sanctuary director had enclosed and began to read from it. It was the last letter from Billy to his cousin Kani.

My Dear Cousin Kani,

Today is the First Moon Day and ten years since I set foot here in Sanctuary. All that time and no word from you! But I try not to worry because the trunkline say that you are still Bull Council Leader. Keeping in touch has become more and more difficult. Letters are lost with all the confusion and the terrible things that are happening to Elephants and other Animals around the world. But I have faith that you and the Family are well. Like Winston, you were born to be great. Indeed, you have become a legend among all Elephants. I am so proud to call you my cousin and friend.

Nonetheless, I miss you and the Family. Many nights I dream of you all. There we sit together, under the great fig tree, and tell stories like the old days.

Africa, and even the zoo, seem so far away! But since today is our birthday, it seems a grand thing to write and remember happy days!

Life has been good since I came to Sanctuary. There are lots of other Elephants: seven other Bulls and thirty girls. Well, I should say Women Elephants although one, Sweet Sally, is only seventeen! Yes, life is good now.

I have been very lucky. All the time I was left alone in the zoo, I was afraid that I would never see Lucy again. For many years, I felt very guilty. Lucy and I didn't part on such good terms.

She was so depressed and frail by the time she left. And me? Well, I was a self-centered teenager who really didn't understand what she was going through. You know she was really like an Auntie to me. Lucy lost her family long ago, but as Elephant tradition has it, she took me in as an adopted son. I wasn't her real son, nor she my real Auntie, but we Elephants always stick together.

I grew to understand just how Lucy felt and why she didn't want to talk much. Eventually, I too complained about my feet. They became cracked and aching, and my bones – oh, the arthritis does hurt on cold days! And just like Lucy, I took to standing in the exhibit corner, my forehead pressed against the wall, swaying and swaying. Those are sad and terrible times I'd rather forget.

But bad things, as you once said, have the chance to turn into good. On the day that I arrived here in Sanctuary, who should be the first to greet me with trumpets? Lucy herself! Well, an Old Bull like me should be a little embarrassed to admit this, but I will tell you that I shed more than a few tears when we trunk hugged.

Now, after many Wildebeest migrations have passed, I am almost a brand new Elephant! The first month I was here I could hardly walk! But now, I can almost outrun some of the younger Bulls!

Kani, I think even you would enjoy it here. Oh, I know it is still captivity. We live behind fences and we miss our Families. But it is so different from the zoo! The people who care for us are kind hearted and listen to what we want and need. There are wonderful woods and hills and streams! And most important of all, Cousin, there are stars! Kani, I can see stars again!

It had been almost forty years since I had seen that open sky sparkling with stars! I had begun to think that stars weren't real, that perhaps they, like so many memories of mine, were simply childhood fantasies!

I love the peace here. I drink in the delicious quiet like water we sucked up with our trunks as children. Remember your seventh birthday party at the river? When I read about the celebration in your letter, I laughed until my trunk ached hearing how Auntie B. slid all the way down and splashed into the water!

Yes, I laughed, but it didn't last long, Cousin. I loved your letters – I lived for them! I devoured them like sweet pods! Your letters caused a million emotions. There were times when a letter sat unopened for days. I was fearful at what I might learn. I still remember the shock of Winston's terrible death. Every letter brought with it the fear that someone might have been hurt or died.

At the same time, I savored every word. I could pretend I was living in Africa with Grandmama, you, and all the others. I even imagined at times that Ma was still alive and my being sent to the zoo was just a bad nightmare. But it wasn't a dream.

Other letters made me angry and jealous, like the time when you wrote about the great adventures you were having with Mishak. I wanted it to be me, not Mishak, who explored the Savanna with you under midnight blue skies with lions roaring and spears lurking in the shadows! But here I was, locked up in a tiny cell, alone.

At times, I thought I might die of loneliness. Indeed, I think I would have if nice people like Ray and Reggie had not fought long and hard for my release to Sanctuary! That is something that I have learned in captivity, Kani, that perhaps you do not know. Loneliness can kill you as easily as a spear or gun. Without love, my heart began to crack like the African earth when rain does not come. But as luck would have it, the Sanctuary took me in and here I am writing you yet another long letter and celebrating another birthday! These days I am a lazy Elephant indeed! Some days I just stand by the pond playing in the water, listening to the Birds sing. We even have Hornbills – well, they call them Wild Turkeys here, but they are very much the same. Great big beautiful tails, very sensitive, and wise. . .

Here, Billy's letter stopped. Then it began again. But the writing looked different, less certain and less clear.

Cousin Kani, I got distracted! I didn't finish my letter to you! Since I last wrote, two new Elephants have arrived. It is always a grand occasion with much trumpeting, chirping, and good time all round. Well, I had better close for now. I'm feeling a little tired and think I will walk up to the Great Oak and watch some stars. I will write more tomorrow. Be well, dear Cousin. It is my honor to be able to call such a Great Bull as you my friend and cousin. Sending many glad trumpets to the Family.

Ever Your Cousin,
Imenti

There Imenti's letter ended, but the Sanctuary director had written a postscript.

P.S. Mr. Kani, there is something else that I am sending. As you will see, the package contains Billy's jawbone. One day, he asked me to promise to return one of his bones to Africa. He also told me that his real Elephant name was Imenti, and that Billy was the name the zoo had given him. "This way," he explained, "when you return my bones, Imenti will be back home in Africa again."

Now my promise is fulfilled. May you and your Family live in peace and prosperity.

Reggie

Umkhulu, who was none other than Kani, stopped reading. By now, night had passed into day. The moon and stars disappeared as the sun began to take his place in the morning sky. Many of the young Elephants sitting around the Old Bull had tears running down their trunks and faces.

Silently, placing the last letters back into the envelope, Kani drew out the half-moon shaped jawbone of his cousin Imenti. He then laid it upon the ground beside the brown parcel. Closing his eyes, Kani gently ran his trunk along the curved surface of the bone. A smile appeared on the Old Bull's face. Suddenly, the air filled with music. It was the Song of the Savanna! Imenti was home.

Dear Reader,

Hello! I am very happy that you have gotten to meet Billy and Kani. *The Elephant Letters* was written to bring the story of the Elephants to children around the world. As a scientist and animal advocate, I have devoted my life to helping animals heal from the violence inflicted upon them by Humans. Our non-profit organization, The Kerulos Center, was created to spread the word that we are brothers and sisters with all Animals. Our motto is "kin under skin, fin, feather and fur" because science - and our hearts - tell us what children already know: all Animals deserve love, respect and dignity.

The characters of Billy and Kani are based on what science tells us about Elephants in the wild and in captivity. The experiences of the two cousins show that the problems of Elephant poaching, habitat destruction, and the soul-crushing isolation in zoos and circuses are very real.

The Elephants and other Animals need your help. You can make a difference in the lives of all Animals by sharing what you have learned from reading *The Elephant Letters*. The Kerulos Center's Billy and Kani Fund was created to empower children to change the way Humans see and feel about other Animals. We invite you to our website to learn more about Elephants and how we can join hands and trunks to restore peace and harmony on our beautiful planet.

I look forward to hearing your ideas on how we can create a loving world for everyone.

Trumpets to you,
Dr. Gay Bradshaw
The Billy and Kani Fund
The Kerulos Center
www.kerulos.org

THE BILLY & KANI FUND

ABOUT THE AUTHOR

G.A. Bradshaw (gabradshaw.com) holds doctorates in both ecology and psychology. She is author of *Elephants on the Edge: What Animals Teach Us About Humanity* (Yale 2009) and the scientist who first identified post-traumatic stress disorder (PTSD) in free living African Elephants. Dr. Bradshaw is the founder and director of The Kerulos Center (www.kerulos.org) and lives with her trans-species family in Southern Oregon where they care for The Tortoise and Hare Sanctuary.

ACKNOWLEDGMENTS

Many thanks to Lorraine Donlon for her support and cover design, Laurel Briggs (creativemdesign.com) for the lovely layout, Steve Passiouras of bookow.com for the beautiful final adjustments to the cover and interior, and my dear friends and Elephant supporters for their help. Finally, I would like to thank Jeff Borchers, my family and all the other Animals of the world for being who they are and O. Mein Gans, forever.